ALL ABOUT...

THE

SECOND WORLD WAR
1939-1945

PAM ROBSON

First published in Great Britain by Macdonald Young Books

Reprinted in 2002 and 2004 by Hodder Wayland,
an imprint of Hodder Children's Books
Reprinted in 2006 by Wayland, an imprint of Hachette Children's Books

© Wayland 1996

A CIP catalogue for this book is available from the British Library.

ISBN-10: 0 7500 2147 0
ISBN-13: 978 0 7500 2147 0

Editor: Annie Scothern
Designer: Jane Hannath
Picture credits: Peter Newark's Historical Pictures - *10,11t, 19b, 26t, 28b, 35,
37t, 44t.* Peter Topham - *6t, 8b, 26b, 40, 44b.* BBC Worldwide - *6b.* Bridgeman - *8t.*
Popperfoto - *9t, 14t, 24, 31t.* Mary Evans Picture Library - *9b, 17b, 19t, 32, 39b.*
Wayland - *11b, 21r, 30t, 41.* Hulton Deutsch - *12, 20, 21t, 23t, 25, 28t, 39t, 45.*
Corbis - *13, 31b.* Imperial War Museum - *14b, 15t, 29, 36/37, 42.* Cabinet War Rooms -
25b. English Heritage - *17l.* Ronald Grant Archive - *22.* Camera Press - *33.*
National Maritime Museum - *34.* Robert Harding - *43.* Peter Newark's Military Pictures - *cover.*

The author and publishers thank the above for permission to reproduce their photographs.

Printed in China

Titles in the ALL ABOUT... series:
ANCIENT GREECE
THE FIRST WORLD WAR
THE GREAT FIRE OF LONDON
THE INDUSTRIAL REVOLUTION
THE SECOND WORLD WAR
THE TUDORS
THE VICTORIANS

Wayland, an imprint of Hachette Children's Books
338 Euston Road, London NWI 3BH

ALL ABOUT...

THE

SECOND WORLD WAR

1939-1945

PAM ROBSON

WILLS'S CIGARETTES

WILLS'S CIGARETTES

WILLS'S CIGARETTES

GLOUCESTER GAUNTLET
INTERCEPTOR FIGHTERS

PILOTS RUNNING TO MACHINES
TO TAKE OFF

REPRESENTATION OF BALLOON
BARRAGE FOR DEFENCE OF LONDON

WILLS'S CIGARETTES

ANTI-AIRCRAFT SEARCHLIGHT

WAYLAND

TIMELINE

1914-18 *The Great War, also known as the First World War*
1933 January *Adolf Hitler becomes Chancellor of Germany*
1938 September *Britain and Germany sign the Munich Accord*

1939 1 September *Germany sweeps into Poland*
     3 September *Britain and France declare war on Germany*

1940 May *Winston Churchill is made Prime Minister of Britain*
     10 May *The Germans sweep into Belgium and the
       Netherlands*
     26 May-2 June *Evacuation of British and French troops
       from Dunkirk*
     22 June *France signs an armistice with Germany*
     13 August *The Battle of Britain begins*
     7 September *The Blitz begins*

1941 June *Germany invades Russia*
     7 December *Japan bombs Pearl Harbour*
     11 December *Germany and Italy declare war on USA*

1942 November *British victory at El Alamein*

1943 February *German defeat at Stalingrad*

1944 6 June *D-Day landings in Normandy*
     Germany attacks Britain with V1 and V2 rockets

1945 12-13 February *Bombing of Dresden*
     8 May *VE (Victory in Europe) Day*
     6 August *First atomic bomb is dropped on Hiroshima*
     24 October *The United Nations organisation (UN) is
      founded*

CONTENTS

REMINDERS OF THE PAST

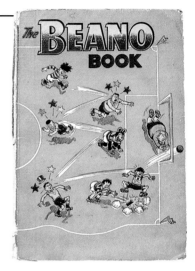

W e can learn about the Second World War at first hand by reading and listening to the recollections of those who were there. We also have other sources of information such as archives and artefacts.

In 1930s Britain, children's comics like the Beano *were favourites.*

The War began in 1939 and for six long years everyone in Britain was involved, civilians as well as the armed forces. The aftermath was as devastating as the War itself.

Radio broadcasting began in Britain in the 1920s.

By 1942 the first nuclear reactor in the world had been built in America as part of the project to make atomic weapons.

In 1949 a time capsule was buried in the foundations of the new Festival Hall in London. The hall was designed to be the centrepiece of the Festival of Britain in 1951, which aimed to create a new postwar spirit of hope among the British people. If a time capsule had been buried in 1939, it would probably have contained images of the new age of technology that was then just beginning – from radio, television and cars to radar and the splitting of the atom.

RADAR is short for RAdio Detecting And Ranging. It works by bouncing high frequency radio waves off solid objects back to a transmitter.

7

LEGACIES OF WAR

Guernica by Picasso

To test their plan to target civilians, German planes bombed Guernica in Spain during the Spanish Civil War. A thousand people died.

The First World War (1914-18) had inspired technological progress, but it had also left behind much poverty. Many social changes had taken place. The harsh peace terms forced on Germany had made the German people angry. Fascism and communism were becoming popular at a time of mass unemployment and starvation. Stalin was forcing communism on to the Russians, while democratic nations like Britain wanted only security and stability.

The game of Monopoly was invented in America during the Depression by an unemployed engineer.

In 1936, unemployed workers in north-east England marched 300 miles from Jarrow to London.

The shock waves of the 1929-34 Depression in America were felt worldwide. Six million unemployed Germans turned to Hitler's Nazi party. In Italy fascism flourished under Mussolini, while

In 1920s Germany, banknotes (Deutschmarks) had so little value that they were sometimes used to paper walls instead of wallpaper. A sackful of notes was needed to buy bread.

Franco's fascists caused civil war in Spain. These legacies from the First World War paved the way for the next world war (1939-45).

NATIONAL SOZIALISTS

After the abdication of Kaiser Wilhelm II in 1918, the Weimar Republic was set up in Germany. The harsh terms of the Treaty of Versailles (1919), soaring inflation and mass unemployment allowed strong new leaders to take charge. Adolf Hitler's National Socialists, or Nazis, became the most powerful group – more through acts of violence than by democratic means. In January 1933 Hitler became Chancellor (Prime Minister) and democracy in Germany no longer existed. Other political groups disappeared.

The 11th Olympic Games were held in Berlin in 1936. The black American Jesse Owens won four medals. He was the star of the games but Hitler refused to speak to him.

To increase the population in Germany, the Cross of Honour of the German Mother was awarded to women who bore several children. Every German, or Aryan, had to prove his or her Aryan background.

Non-Aryans like the Jews were persecuted and many fled from Germany.

Under the Nazis, Germany quickly expanded its territory in Europe. In 1938 Hitler occupied Austria.

By 1935 conscription had been reintroduced. German armies were mobilised just one year later. Worried by this growing aggression, Britain and France began to rearm.

The Nazis were fascists. They wanted Germans to be the most powerful race in Europe. Hitler was called the 'Führer' (leader) and every German household had to have a copy of his book Mein Kampf. *All German children were taught Nazi beliefs.*

Baut Jugendherbergen und Heime

JAPANESE IMPERIALISM

W hile Hitler's armies were occupying countries in Europe, Japan had already taken up arms against China and by 1937 a full-scale war was in progress. America pressured the Japanese to withdraw and in 1941 the Japanese launched a surprise attack against the American fleet at Pearl Harbour in Hawaii. By June 1942 the Japanese had taken British territories in the Far East, including Singapore.

In September 1938 the British Prime Minister, Neville Chamberlain, signed the Anglo-German Accord in Munich. He wanted peace not war. A year later, on 3 September at 11.15 a.m., Chamberlain announced on British radio that war had been declared on Germany.

USA

PACIFIC OCEAN

ATLANTIC OCEAN

HAWAII

Pearl Harbour

SOUTH AMERICA

KEY

Areas of conflict

on land

at sea

The merging of these two arenas of war brought about 'total war'. At first the British and French adopted a policy of appeasement towards Germany. But when the Germans invaded Poland in September 1939, Britain and France finally declared war.

Japanese soldiers guarding Chinese prisoners during the Japanese invasion of Shanghai in 1937

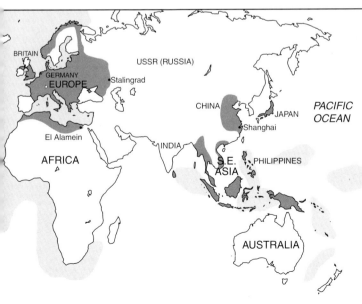

The Second World War extended across Europe, North Africa and South East Asia. The war at sea was fought in both the Atlantic and the Pacific oceans. Britain, Germany and Japan were heavily bombed.

13

BLITZKRIEG!

G ermany had devised a new military strategy called Blitzkrieg, or 'lightning war', that involved a rapid sweep into enemy territory with tanks and air support. On 1 September 1939 Germany swept into Poland.

British people listened to their wireless set (radio) for news of the War.

The Germans had invented the Enigma cipher machine to send secret messages. But Polish, French and British cryptographers broke the cipher in May 1940. The Germans did not realise this until after the War.

FREEDOM SHALL PREVAIL!

The dominions of the British Empire were now the Commonwealth. Troops from places such as Canada, India and West Indies fought alongside the British armed forces.

In Britain preparations for war had already been made and conscription was reintroduced. The British Expeditionary Force (BEF) and light bomber aircraft squadrons headed for France, while the Navy sailed to Scapa Flow in the Orkney Islands. The evacuation of children from urban to rural areas of Britain was put into effect. Winston Churchill joined the new War Cabinet as First Lord of the Admiralty. By May 1940 he was Prime Minister. On 17 September 1939, Russia invaded Poland. Ten days later a friendship treaty was signed by Germany and Russia that divided Poland between them.

The underground Cabinet War Rooms in London provided protection for the British government against air attack. British war operations were directed from there.

'SITZKRIEG'

F rom September 1939 until May 1940, British and French forces remained on the defensive in Europe. This time of waiting was nicknamed 'sitzkrieg'. On 10 May German forces swept into the neutral territories of Belgium and the Netherlands. Civilians were targeted in air raids and by 15 May the Dutch had surrendered. Belgium fought on for three more weeks.

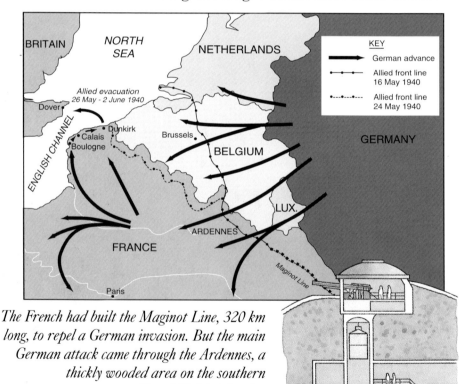

The French had built the Maginot Line, 320 km long, to repel a German invasion. But the main German attack came through the Ardennes, a thickly wooded area on the southern French/Belgian border.

During the Second World War, British naval headquarters were based in a network of tunnels below Dover Castle on the south-east coast of England. The evacuation of Dunkirk was masterminded from there.

British and French troops – the 'Allies' – advanced through Belgium to defend the Channel ports. But German forces broke through the Allied front line and moved north towards the coast. The Allies were cornered at Dunkirk and a massive evacuation of troops across the Channel to England began. By 22 June the French had signed an armistice with Germany and Britain stood alone against Hitler's Nazis.

A fleet of civilian boats crossed the English Channel to help with the evacuation from Dunkirk.

BATTLE OF THE ATLANTIC

C onflict began in the Atlantic Ocean soon after war was declared and continued throughout the next six years. The Allies needed to keep shipping lanes open and blockade German ports. Many British beaches were fenced off to stop the Germans landing. German 'wolfpacks' of U-boat submarines harassed and sank British ships travelling in convoys. These ships were carrying vital supplies of oil, food, machinery and raw materials. In the Atlantic, radar was vital both for offensive and defensive measures.

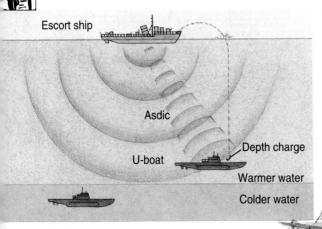

Escort ship

Asdic

Depth charge

U-boat

Warmer water

Colder water

'Asdic' was a short-range echo sounder that was used by Allied ships to locate enemy submarines.

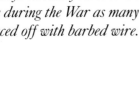

Seaside holidays virtually came to an end in Britain during the War as many beaches were fenced off with barbed wire.

Atlantic convoys were under attack from above and below.

Air cover was essential and aircraft carriers were to prove a key factor in sea battles, especially in the Pacific. Aircraft could now detect U-boats with radar. By 1943, 238 U-boats had been sunk.

Aircraft carriers made it possible for combatants to fight without ever sighting each other.

A 'PHONEY' WAR

Hitler wanted a quick victory in Europe, 'total war' was not in his plans. There was some rationing in Germany in 1939-40 but German women had not yet been encouraged to go out to work for the war effort. However, listening to foreign radio broadcasts was forbidden and German schoolchildren were being taught about the superiority of the Aryan race.

Anti-gas measures had already been planned in Britain two years before war was declared.

As Allied soldiers joked about the 'sitzkrieg' in Europe, British children were being evacuated to the countryside.

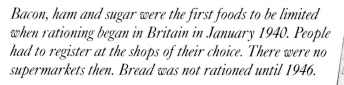

Bacon, ham and sugar were the first foods to be limited when rationing began in Britain in January 1940. People had to register at the shops of their choice. There were no supermarkets then. Bread was not rationed until 1946.

In Britain the Air Raid Precautions (ARP) system had been established in 1935. By October 1939 every British adult carried a green identity card. Under-16s carried a beige card. Ration books were issued in September 1939. Gas masks were distributed, but to the British people it seemed more like a 'phoney war' than a real war between September 1939 and May 1940.

Many British families went into Anderson shelters during air raids.

21

THE BATTLE OF BRITAIN

I n May 1940, British volunteers joined Home Guard units. These were to be the last line of defence against Hitler's forces. A German invasion was expected in September 1940. Hitler's plan, code-named Operation Sealion, was to land troops on the south coast of England. But first Hitler aimed to wipe out British Fighter Command – the only force left that was capable of attacking his armies. On 13 August 1940 the German air force, the Luftwaffe, began its attack.

Churchill first used the title 'Home Guard' in July 1940. By 1943 nearly two million men had joined this 'dad's army'. A TV series was later made called Dad's Army.

Maps of Britain were withdrawn and signposts were disguised to confuse any invading Germans.

Fighter pilots from places such as Canada, Poland, West Indies and Australia fought alongside British pilots. Of the 3,080 aircrew who flew with Fighter Command during the Battle of Britain, 520 died.

The targets were airfields, radar stations, ports and aircraft factories. By 7 September London had become the target. On 17 September Operation Sealion was postponed indefinitely. The use of radar had helped the British to track Luftwaffe raiders and to scramble fighter bombers at speed to intercept them.

Churchill said of the Battle of Britain: "Never in the field of human conflict was so much owed by so many to so few."

23

THE BLITZ

I t was thought that poisonous gas would be the
weapon that would be used against civilians in the
1939-45 war. In fact it was the bomb. From
7 September 1940 until 16 May 1941, British cities
and industrial centres were targeted continuously by
Luftwaffe bombers. Warning sirens wailed almost
constantly as London endured 57 consecutive nights of
bombing between
7 September and
2 November, and further
heavy raids followed.

*Over two million British
homes were damaged by
German parachute
mines.*

Until 1943, barrage balloons played an important part in British air defence. The idea was that the propellers of enemy planes would get caught in the balloons' ropes.

Of the 15 other British cities attacked, Coventry in the Midlands suffered the most extensive damage. During this period, now known as the 'Blitz', 41,000 civilians were killed and 137,000 injured. Contrary to Hitler's hopes, the Blitz made the British people even more determined to win the War.

Coventry Cathedral was severely damaged by German bombs.

Londoners often sheltered in the Underground stations during air raids.

CIVIL DEFENCE

C ivilian life in Britain continued as usual wherever possible, often with much good humour displayed. When fire bombs set cities alight, this was no easy task. In 1941 it became essential to set up a National Fire Service (NFS).

Each local authority in Britain had its own fire service, with a range of firefighting equipment. When the NFS was set up, firefighting equipment was standardised.

WILLS'S CIGARETTES

LIGHT TRAILER FIRE-PUMP

Smoking cigarettes was very popular then. Children collected picture cards from cigarette packets. Wartime activities were often featured.

WILLS'S CIGARETTES

A CHAIN OF BUCKETS

By 1943 almost two million volunteers had joined the civil defence organisations – ARP, fire, ambulance and police services. Air raid wardens reported all bombings and decided the nature of the help needed. There were unexploded

WILLS'S CIGARETTES

TWO-MEN PORTABLE MANUAL FIRE-PUMP IN ACTION

bombs to be defused; people buried alive beneath fallen buildings to be dug out; and the homeless to be looked after. Mobile food canteens appeared in the debris-strewn streets.

Men and women worked together to help the injured.

CIVIL DEFENCE

F (JP) W

WVS REST CENTRE

SAVE AND MEND

D aily life in Britain was subject to government restrictions. These were designed to share out all resources equally and avoid waste. People were encouraged to 'dig for victory' and

Women in the Land Army helped to keep Britain supplied with vegetables.

many had allotments where they grew vegetables.

The sweets ration in Britain was increased from 50g to 75g a week in 1942. Liquid paraffin was used as an ingredient in cakes. Milk powder and dried eggs were introduced in 1943. Some foods like fish and bananas were rarely seen.

Covered in swastikas (the emblem of Nazi Germany), Squander Bug was a cartoon character used to persuade Britons not to waste anything.

Farmers worked day and night to grow more food. Many women joined the Land Army. In June 1941 clothes rationing began and old clothes had to be recycled. By November 1941 a points rationing system had been introduced that gave everyone 16 points a month, as well as the ordinary rations. These points could be used on anything, even canned food like American 'Spam'. Soon raw materials were in short supply and recycling paper, glass and aluminium became vital.

By June 1940 vegetables were even growing in the Tower of London moat! Canned fruit and vegetables appeared in the shops.

Women at War

In 1939, British men between the ages of 18 and 41 were conscripted. By 1941 the upper age limit had been raised to 51 and, for the first time, unmarried women between the ages of 19 and 30 had also been conscripted. Eventually all British women up to the age of 50 had to register for war work. By June 1944, 16 million Britons were occupied in civilian war work, while 4.5 million men and 0.5 million women were in the British armed forces. The mass production of aircraft and weapons, or munitions work, was a high priority.

The 'siren suit' became a popular thing for women to wear in wartime Britain.

Munitions work was extremely dangerous but there was often a good community spirit among the workers. The women wore badges like the one shown here (ROF stands for Royal Ordnance Factory).

Some women made barrage balloons.

Conscripted women could choose to go into industry or join forces such as the Land Army and the Women's Auxiliary Airforce (WAAF). When barrage balloons were phased out in 1943, the WAAFs responsible for their maintenance were retrained as flight mechanics.

Women in the Air Transport Auxiliary (ATA) ferried aircraft from factories to airfields. The famous pilot Amy Johnson was killed ferrying a Spitfire. Today women can fly combat aircraft in action.

31

HOT DESERTS, COLD PLAINS

I n September 1940 the Italians invaded Egypt. By
February 1941 the British had inflicted heavy defeats
on them but then the German Afrika Korps, led by
Rommel, were victorious. Egypt was under threat
again. In November 1942 Montgomery led the British
Eighth Army to victory at El Alamein after a
month of fighting. By September 1943 Italy had
surrendered. On the Eastern Front the treaty
between Russia and Germany ended abruptly
when Hitler invaded Russia in June 1941.

*German troops surrendered to the Russians
at Stalingrad in 1943. In the bitter cold, the
Germans wore straw overboots.*

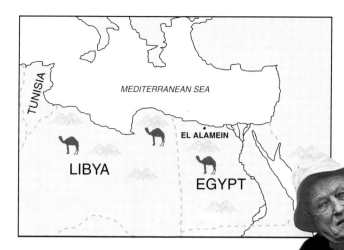

MEDITERRANEAN SEA

TUNISIA

LIBYA

EGYPT

EL ALAMEIN

The author Roald Dahl was a fighter pilot in the Libyan desert in North Africa. His nose was smashed and his back damaged when his plane crash-landed in the sand.

Mrs Churchill immediately launched the Aid to Russia fund, despite the British fear of communism. In February 1943 the Germans surrendered to the Russians at Stalingrad. The Russians then marched towards Poland in a costly campaign. By the end of the War, Russia had the highest number of casualties.

This Grant tank was used at El Alamein by Lieutenant General Montgomery, known as 'Monty'. The main gun is in the hull not in the turret.

33

PEARL HARBOUR

Fortunately the American aircraft carriers were not in Pearl Harbour when the attack occurred. This was to prove vital to USA victory in the Pacific in 1945.

On 7 December 1941, without warning, 363 Japanese aircraft attacked the American fleet anchored in Pearl Harbour in Hawaii. The next day the American president, Roosevelt, declared war on Japan. On 11 December Germany and Italy declared war on the USA. Two separate arenas of war had merged into 'total war'. Churchill and Roosevelt agreed to deal with Germany first.

The two sides in the Second World War were known as the Allied powers and the Axis powers. By the spring of 1942, most of Europe was under German occupation.

In August 1942 America joined the Allied air offensive with daylight bombing raids over Germany. By January 1943 a combined British/American bombing campaign was underway. Radar had been further improved and specific targets could now be located. By spring 1944 Berlin had been destroyed. A massive Allied invasion of Europe was already planned.

The British Lancaster plane

During an Allied air raid over Hamburg in which 30,000 people died, clouds of aluminium strips called 'window' were dropped to block the German aircraft tracking system.

D-DAY, 6 JUNE 1944

A fter five years of war, occupied Europe – fortified by the German Atlantic Wall and the Siegfried Line – seemed impregnable to the Allies. But on 6 June 1944, after two years of secret planning, liberation was in sight. The Allied invasion of Europe was code-named Operation Overlord. In southern England armoured vehicles headed for the coast. D-Day arrived. The sea was rough and when the assault forces arrived in France many troops were suffering from seasickness.

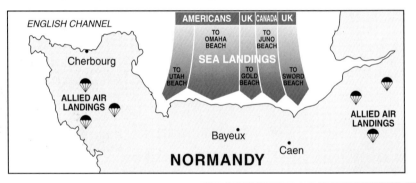

ENGLISH CHANNEL

AMERICANS | UK | CANADA | UK

TO OMAHA BEACH | TO JUNO BEACH

SEA LANDINGS

TO UTAH BEACH | TO GOLD BEACH | TO SWORD BEACH

Cherbourg

ALLIED AIR LANDINGS

ALLIED AIR LANDINGS

Bayeux

Caen

NORMANDY

The five invasion beaches were each given a name. On D-Day (the day that Operation Overlord began) 4,000 landing craft were escorted by 600 warships with 10,000 Allied aircraft providing air support. Montgomery commanded the assault forces. This is a panel (right) from the Overlord Embroidery.

Planning for Operation Overlord had begun in 1942. An appeal for holiday photographs of the invasion beaches in Normandy was broadcast on British radio.

Gustav the pigeon flew back to Britain with details of the D-Day landings and was later awarded the Dickin Medal.

Fog and heavy cloud reduced visibility for air support. On that first day 156,000 British, Canadian and American troops were landed on the beaches of Normandy. Eleven months later Germany surrendered. The element of surprise had been achieved by tricking the enemy beforehand.

Inflatable tanks were one of many tricks used to make Hitler think an Allied invasion would take place further up the French coast near Calais.

37

CITIES DESTROYED

War continued for some months after D-Day. From June 1944 until March 1945, Britain was terrorised by Hitler's deadly new rocket bombs – the V1, or 'doodlebug', and the V2. These long-range ballistic missiles were designed by the scientist who later helped the Americans send the first men to the moon. At Christmas 1944 Britain shivered beneath a blanket of snow and freezing fog but the children were

In June 1944 an average of 50 doodlebugs hit London every day.

allowed an extra sweets ration. This was Britain's last Christmas at war but rationing continued for some time. In February 1945 the British RAF dropped 2,690 tonnes of bombs from over 700 aircraft on to the German city of Dresden at night.

Peter the dog was awarded the Dickin Medal for saving six people buried alive after doodlebug attacks.

38

After the Allied bombings in February 1945, most of Dresden lay in ruins.

Fires were seen for 100 miles and many thousands of people were killed. As daylight came a further raid was made by the Americans.

The Frauenkirche in Dresden is now being rebuilt. A golden orb and cross, a symbol of peace, will be placed on the top. This is to be paid for by the British.

Although carrying a 1,000 kg warhead, the German V2 rocket arrived unseen and unheard. V2s hit London almost every day in December 1944.

VICTIMS OF WAR

I n Burma the Japanese used prisoners of war (POWs) to build the infamous 'death railway'. Colditz Castle in Germany was used as a high-security POW camp for Allied officers. In August 1944, with jubilant cheers ringing in their ears, the Americans liberated Paris. On 15 April 1945, to the sound of silence, British troops liberated Belsen, a German concentration camp. The appalling scenes witnessed in Belsen arouse horror even today, over 50 years later. At least 60,000 Jews were imprisoned in Belsen. Hundreds died daily from starvation and disease.

Anne Frank and her family were Jewish. They hid from the Nazis in an attic in the Netherlands until they were betrayed. Anne died in Belsen aged only 16. Her diary was published and we can still read it today.

Resistance groups in occupied countries helped the Allied troops during liberation.

The Allied liberation force witnessed horrifying scenes inside the concentration camps.

Each week every POW was sent a Red Cross parcel. The International Red Cross was started by Henri Dunant.

Nazi concentration camps were set up in most of the occupied countries. In Poland extermination camps systematically killed six million Jews.

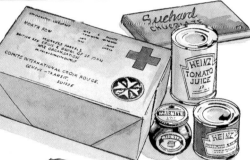

Around 61,000 Allied POWs and 250,000 civilians were used as slave labour to build the Burma-Siam 'death railway', which was needed by the Japanese to transport supplies. Some 16,000 POWs died from the brutal treatment they received.

THE FINAL BOMB

I n January 1945 the Russians liberated Poland, replacing Nazi occupation with communism. On 9 February the Allies broke through the Siegfried Line, Germany's last line of defence. On 8 May thousands of Britons celebrated the Allied victory in Europe with VE Day parties. Hitler had committed suicide but other leading Nazis were tried for war crimes. Japan battled on. Roosevelt died in April and Truman took over as American president.

Parties took place in the streets of Britain on VE (Victory in Europe) Day.

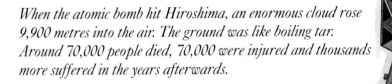

When the atomic bomb hit Hiroshima, an enormous cloud rose 9,900 metres into the air. The ground was like boiling tar. Around 70,000 people died, 70,000 were injured and thousands more suffered in the years afterwards.

Truman brought the War to a close by ordering the bombing of the Japanese city of Hiroshima with an atomic bomb. At 8.15 a.m. on 6 August 1945, the bomb was released by the B-29 bomber *Enola Gay*. It took 53 seconds to fall. The shock wave shook the plane. A second atomic bomb was then dropped on the city of Nagasaki. On 2 September Japan surrendered unconditionally.

The bomb Little Boy *hit Hiroshima on 6 August 1945.*

43

THE AFTERMATH

F ifty countries signed the 1945 United Nations Charter, with the aim of preventing future wars. America's Marshall Plan provided the money to rebuild Europe. The four Allied powers – Britain, America, Russia and France – occupied and divided Germany into two countries. Then a different kind of war began, which became known as the Cold War. This was between the two major powers that had emerged out of the Second World War – America and Russia.

The Festival of Britain in 1951 aimed to create a new postwar spirit of hope among the British people.

The Berlin Wall divided Germany's old capital, Berlin. It was pulled down in 1989. The following year Germany became one country again.

Temporary houses, or 'prefabs', were put up in Britain while new towns were being built to rehouse people bombed out of their homes.

Split into East and West, Germany became the front line of the Cold War. Only the deterrent of atomic power prevented another war. Today Germany is one country again and is part of the European Community. Russia had become known as the USSR as communism spread. Today democracy is being restored and the USSR has broken up. The Cold War is over.

MILITARY DEATHS 1939-45	
Britain & Commonwealth	420,000
France	245,000
Germany	4,200,000
Italy	395,000
Japan	1,972,000
USA	298,000
USSR	18,000,000

Estimates of total deaths in the Second World War vary between 50 and 60 million people. But it is known that more civilians died than troops. Each year on Remembrance Sunday in November, Britain remembers the dead of both world wars.

GLOSSARY

Aryan *A term used by the Nazis to describe German Caucasians of non-Jewish descent.*

atom (or atomic) bomb *A bomb from which energy is released by nuclear fission, or the splitting of an atomic nucleus.*

Berlin Wall *After defeat in 1945, Germany was divided into East and West. The old capital, Berlin, lay inside East Germany, which was controlled by communist Russia. Berlin had to be divided by a wall. This wall came down in 1989.*

cipher or cypher *Secret writing where letters are substituted according to a key.*

communism *A movement that aims to establish a society where everyone is equal. In communist Russia this meant a loss of personal freedom for millions of people.*

cryptographer *A person who solves codes and ciphers.*

democracy *Government by the people or their elected representatives.*

Dickin Medal *A Victoria Cross for animals. Each medal has the inscription: 'For gallantry, we also serve'.*

Enigma *The main machine used by the Germans to encode secret messages.*

fascism *A political system that does not allow any opposition. Fascism is the opposite of democracy.*

Führer *A German word meaning leader. Hitler became Führer in 1934.*

Luftwaffe *The German air force.*

Maginot Line *An ineffective line of fortifications built by France on its border with Germany.*

Mein Kampf *The autobiographical book written by Hitler which contained his plans for Germany. In it he describes the Jews as Germany's enemy.*

Nazi *A member of Hitler's National Socialist political party.*

Overlord Embroidery *The modern equivalent of the Bayeux Tapestry. It shows Operation Overlord and can be seen at the D-Day Museum in Portsmouth.*

prefab *A small house assembled quickly from ready-made sections.*

Siegfried Line *The German line of fortifications built along the western border of Germany before the War.*

swastika *The emblem of the Nazi party. It has four clockwise arms bent at right angles. It is also an ancient symbol of peace.*

INDEX